Because of its impressive beauty, Paris, the capital of France, is also called the City of Light.

It's a place where you can find tasty food, incredible architecture, and fantastic art.

A sidewalk cafe in Paris is a relaxing place to sit back and enjoy moments of leisure.

For centuries, writers and
artists have praised Paris.
Many people have relocated to
Paris for the love of the city.

Every year, Paris attracts
numerous admiring visitors.
Paris is a capital of fashion and style.
It is also a hub of finance,
commerce, and industry.

The Eiffel Tower is Paris's most famous landmark.
For the 1889 Paris World's Fair, France erected this lacy iron tower.

The World's Fair commemorated
the 100th anniversary
of the French Revolution,
which started in Paris.

The Eiffel Tower reaches a height
of nearly 1,000 feet (300 meters).
Visitors can reach the top through elevators.

The tower was the world's tallest structure at the time it was constructed. The Eiffel Tower was named after its talented designer Gustave Eiffel.

The river Seine flows through Paris,
dividing Paris in half.
The Right Bank refers to the region
of Paris on the north bank of the river.

The Left Bank refers to the area on the south side of the river.

The Left Bank is home to several government buildings and the University of Paris.

The university is centrally located
in the famous Latin Quarter.
The neighborhood got its name
from students at the university
who spoke Latin.

The Right Bank is home to the majority of Paris' companies and big shops.

The Île de la Cité, an island in the Seine,
is home to the oldest places of Paris.

The famous Notre Dame Cathedral is located on the island.

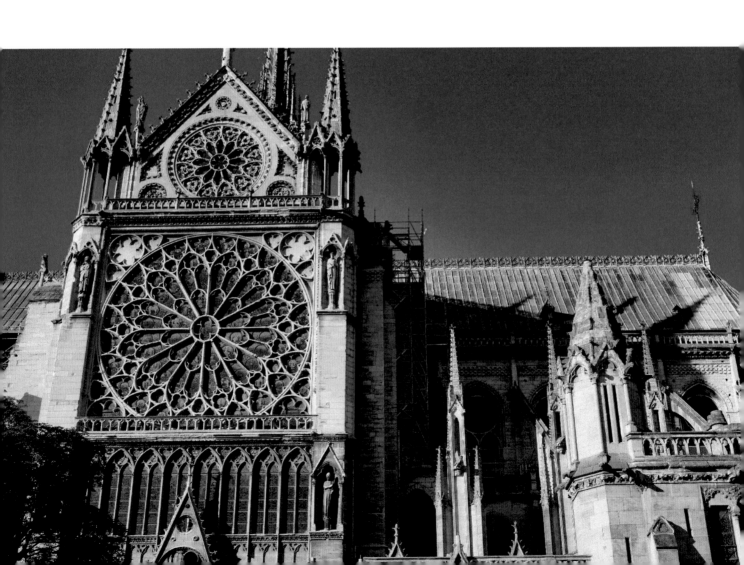

The construction of Notre Dame Cathedral
began in the 12th century;
however, it was not completed
for another 300 years.

Notre Dame is well-known for
its stained-glass windows,
stone gargoyles, and massive stone supports.

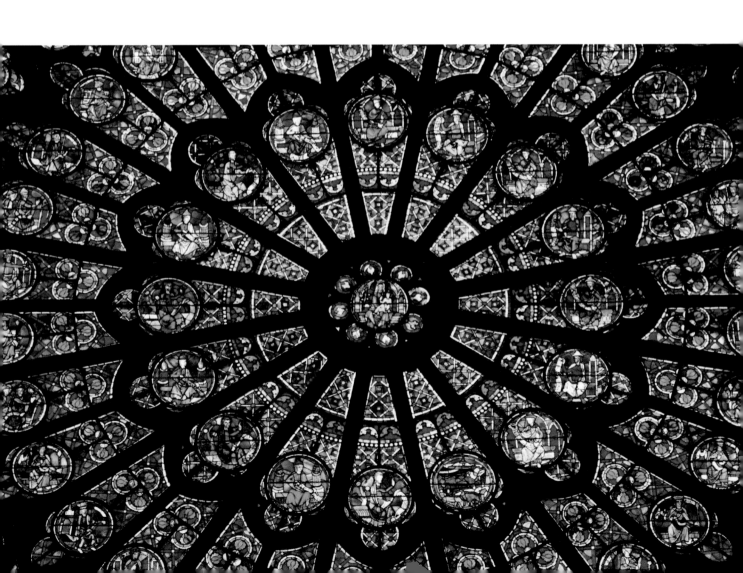

The Sainte-Chapelle, built in the 1200s, is the other church on the Île de la Cité. Built by Louis IX of France to house religious artifacts, Sainte-Chapelle also features stunning stained-glass windows.

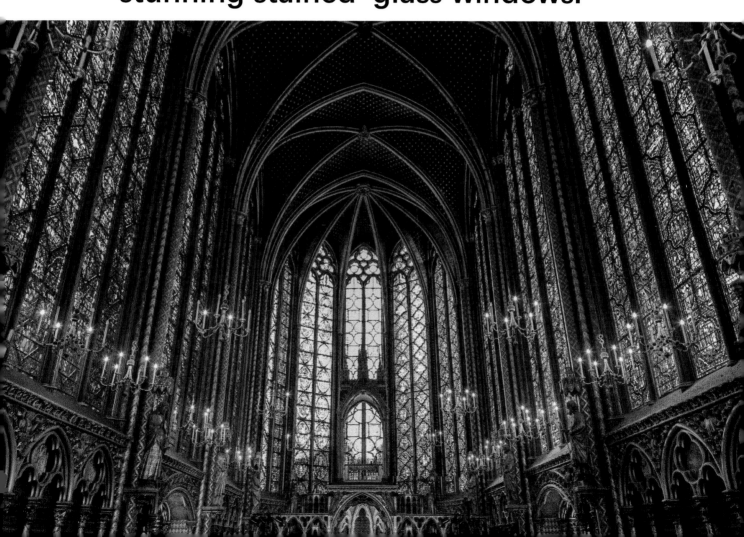

There are many must-see spots in Paris for visitors.

Champs-Élysées is perhaps one of the most famous streets in the world. This broad, tree-lined avenue is lined with chic restaurants, shops, and boutiques.

The Arc de Triomphe (Arch of Triumph) stands at one end of the Champs-Élysées.

This monument was erected to commemorate the triumphs of the French emperor Napoleon I.

At the opposite end is
the Place de la Concorde (Peace Square),
which features giant fountains and statues.

The Louvre is a historical palace located in the heart of Paris.

It's also one of the best-known
museums in the world.
The Mona Lisa, a famous painting
by Leonardo da Vinci, is on display.

If you enjoy impressionist paintings,
make a point of visiting the Musée d'Orsay.
This museum was once a train station.

Despite its size, Paris has numerous parks.
Parisians and tourists alike love unwinding
among the flowers and sculptures
in the Tuileries Gardens,
which are near the Palace de la Concorde.

Rest for a while in one of Paris's lovely parks when you're tired. On the Right Bank are the Tuileries Gardens, and on the Left Bank are the Luxembourg Gardens.

The Palace of Versailles is situated in the suburbs of Paris,
about 12 miles from the city center;
you will need to take the train to get there.

Paris has numerous bridges that were constructed
at various times and in a variety of styles.
Pont Neuf, or New Bridge,
is the oldest bridge, which was completed in 1604.

For hundreds of years, Paris has been
regarded as the cultural capital
of the western world
due to its abundance of theatres,
museums, concert halls, and art galleries.

Numerous writers and scholars
from around the world
have traveled to Paris
to immerse themselves in
the city's culture and beauty.

Famous artists who have lived in Paris included Pablo Picasso and Claude Monet.

Made in the USA
Las Vegas, NV
22 February 2024

86140310R00021